Community Helpers at Work

A Day with a Teacher

By Katie Kawa

Cavendish Square
New York

Published in 2021 by Cavendish Square Publishing, LLC
243 5th Avenue, Suite 136, New York, NY 10016

Copyright © 2021 by Cavendish Square Publishing, LLC

First Edition

No part of this publication may be reproduced, stored in a retrieval system, or transmitted in any form or by any means—electronic, mechanical, photocopying, recording, or otherwise—without the prior permission of the copyright owner. Request for permission should be addressed to Permissions, Cavendish Square Publishing, 243 5th Avenue, Suite 136, New York, NY 10016. Tel (877) 980-4450; fax (877) 980-4454.

Website: cavendishsq.com

This publication represents the opinions and views of the author based on his or her personal experience, knowledge, and research. The information in this book serves as a general guide only. The author and publisher have used their best efforts in preparing this book and disclaim liability rising directly or indirectly from the use and application of this book.

Library of Congress Cataloging-in-Publication Data

Names: Kawa, Katie, author.
Title: A day with a teacher / Katie Kawa.
Description: First edition. | New York : Cavendish Square Publishing, [2021] |
Series: Community helpers at work | Includes index.
Identifiers: LCCN 2019047393 (print) | LCCN 2019047394 (ebook) |
ISBN 9781502658289 (library binding) | ISBN 9781502658265 (paperback) |
ISBN 9781502658272 (set) | ISBN 9781502658296 (ebook)
Subjects: LCSH: Teachers–Juvenile literature. | Lesson planning–Juvenile literature. |
Grading and marking (Students)–Juvenile literature.
Classification: LCC LB1775 .K39 2021 (print) | LCC LB1775 (ebook) |
DDC 371.1–dc23
LC record available at https://lccn.loc.gov/2019047393
LC ebook record available at https://lccn.loc.gov/2019047394

Editor: Katie Kawa
Copy Editor: Nathan Heidelberger
Designer: Andrea Davison-Bartolotta

The photographs in this book are used by permission and through the courtesy of: Cover, pp. 9, 11, 13 Monkey Business Images/Shutterstock.com; pp. 5, 19, 21 wavebreakmedia/Shutterstock.com; p. 7 PeopleImages/E+/Getty Images; p. 15 (bottom) oliveromg/Shutterstock.com; p. 15 (top) JoHo/Shutterstock.com; p. 17 Tempura/E+/Getty Images; p. 21 andresr/E+/Getty Images.

Some of the images in this book illustrate individuals who are models. The depictions do not imply actual situations or events.

CPSIA compliance information: Batch #CS20CSQ: For further information contact Cavendish Square Publishing LLC, New York, New York, at 1-877-980-4450.

Printed in the United States of America

CONTENTS

In the Classroom	4
Learning Different Things	10
An Important Job	16
Words to Know	24
Index	24

In the Classroom

Teachers are an important part of their **community**. They work at schools. They teach people about reading, math, and many other things. The people they teach are called students.

A teacher makes a plan for each day at school. This is called a lesson plan. They follow their lesson plan carefully. This helps them make sure their students are learning everything they need to know.

Teachers get to school early. They set up their classroom for the day. Then, they **greet** their students. Teachers check to see who's at school and who stayed home sick.

Learning Different Things

Teachers read stories to their students. Story time is fun! Teachers also help their students learn to read on their own. They teach their students what sounds each letter makes.

Teachers also help their students learn about numbers. They teach their students about adding and subtracting. Sometimes they write math problems down. They ask their students to find the answers.

Some teachers are art teachers. They help their students draw and **paint**. Other teachers help their students learn about music. They teach them fun songs to sing at school.

An Important Job

Sometimes teachers give their students homework. Teachers have their own homework to do too! They look at their students' homework and tests and give them **grades**. The grades show how well a student is doing at school.

17

Schools often have computers. Teachers help their students learn to use these computers. Teachers also use computers to show videos to their students. Students play learning games on computers too!

Teachers also help students learn outside the classroom. They take their students on field trips. They visit important places in their community. A teacher might plan a field trip to a farm or a zoo to teach students more about animals.

Every teacher has an important job to do. They help their students do well and stay safe at school. They treat their students with kindness and care. Teachers make learning fun!

WORDS TO KNOW

community: An area where people live; a neighborhood.

grades: Numbers or letters that show how well a student did in a class, on a test, or on homework.

greet: To welcome.

paint: To make a picture by using a kind of colored liquid.

INDEX

A
art, 14

C
classroom, 8, 20
community, 4, 20
computers, 18

F
field trips, 20

H
homework, 16

L
lesson plan, 6

M
math, 4, 12
music, 14

R
reading, 4, 10

24